Gulp

A survivor's guide of hope from Cancer.

By
David Jones-Stanley

GULP

First Edition: 2025

David Jones-Stanley

David Jones-Stanley

Author's Note

This is not a medical book. I'm not a doctor, a nurse, or anyone with a certificate on the wall that lets me prescribe you drugs.

What I am is someone who's been through it, the "you have cancer" conversation, the appointments, the scans, the endless waiting, the good days and the ones that break you in half.

When I was diagnosed with oesophageal cancer at 46, I wanted something that told me the truth. Not the neat, brochure, friendly version. Not the kind of "inspirational" story that leaves out the bits where you're swearing at the toaster because you can't swallow your breakfast. I wanted to know what it really feels like, the ridiculous, the terrifying, the hopeful, and the downright absurd.

So that's what this is. My story, unfiltered. Sometimes funny, sometimes heavy, and always honest. If it helps you feel less alone, more prepared, or even just makes you laugh when you thought you couldn't, then it's done its job.

The process of writing was as much about healing as it was about storytelling. These lessons weren't obvious in the middle of treatment, or even in the first months after. They only revealed themselves slowly, as life settled into its "new normal."

If you read this book and feel you're not moving forward as quickly as you hoped, please know this: growth isn't instant. Healing takes time. And that's not failure; it's part of the journey.

Now, let's get started.

David Jones-Stanley

GULP

Part 1
Introduction
and Context

"And when I looked around, I saw
it, that look. That unmistakable look
in their eyes."

About me, my life, and why I wrote this book.

I was diagnosed with oesophageal cancer at 46. I was a husband, a father of three, working full, time, trying to keep all the usual plates spinning. And then, cancer.

Not that there's ever a convenient time to be told you have it, but this certainly wasn't mine. Life was already full, already stretched thin, and now everything was about to be reshaped around appointments, scans, treatments, uncertainty, and fear.

It was hard. Really hard. Navigating work, being present for my kids, supporting my family while managing the exhausting logistics of cancer care, it all felt like too much. And then there was the added challenge of trying to navigate the healthcare system itself. Whether it's the NHS or another provider, it's a maze, and it doesn't come with a map.

After I finished treatment, I finally had the space to start attending a support group at my local hospital. During my treatment support groups weren't really running, they'd been shut down after COVID, for all the obvious reasons, and hadn't quite restarted. But post-treatment, someone pointed me toward one. I turned up not really knowing what to expect. Just a room, a few chairs, a handful of people, but everything changed for me that day.

There were only two others in the room who had already gone through treatment. The rest were newly diagnosed. And when I looked around, I saw it, that look. That unmistakable look in their eyes. I recognised it instantly because I had worn it too: fear, confusion, vulnerability. That moment when your world has tilted and you're grasping for anything that feels solid.

I'll never forget the expression on their faces. And in that moment, I thought: How can I help?

This book is one way I think I can. It's not a definitive handbook. It's just my story, told honestly, without polish, in the hope that it helps someone else make sense of their own. If sharing my experience can make one person feel less alone, less terrified, or more prepared for the road ahead, then it's worth every word.

I wrote this for the next poor bastard who hears the words "you have cancer" and suddenly doesn't know which way is up.

We're not alone.

GULP

David Jones-Stanley

I'm not a doctor! This is my journey my experience.

As I share my personal journey through oesophageal cancer, I want to emphasise the importance of professional medical guidance. My experiences and insights are rooted in my own observations and feelings, but they are not substitutes for the expert advice provided by healthcare professionals.

The path through a cancer diagnosis is deeply personal and complex, varying, greatly, from one individual to another.

Throughout this book, I aim to offer support, understanding, and encouragement to those who might be navigating similar challenges. However, I want to ensure that you are aware of the critical role that medical professionals play in making sound decisions about your health.

Medical disclaimer.

The content of this book is based on my personal experience and observations during my journey with oesophageal cancer. It's intended to provide insight and support to those facing similar challenges. However, please be aware that I am not a medical professional, and the information presented here should not be considered medical advice.

I strongly encourage readers to consult their healthcare team before making any decisions or changes about their health or treatment. Every individual's medical situation is unique, and only a qualified healthcare provider can offer personalised recommendations tailored to your specific needs.

Your health and wellbeing are of utmost importance; please prioritise professional guidance in your journey.

GULP

Part 2
Diagnosis and Initial Reactions

"I steeled myself for a battle I never wanted but now had no choice but to face."

Diagnosis.

No one ever seemed to mention the "C" word. No, not THAT C word, it's just "Cancer." It's as though saying the word "Cancer" out loud would conjure a genie from a bottle, granting you only bad wishes. Trouble is that the rub of the bottle had already happened long before anyone even dared to whisper the word.

Whether they tiptoed around the word "Cancer" or referred to it more delicately as "The Tumour," it came down to the same thing: I have got a squatter living in my body, cells that have decided to throw a wild party without my permission. They are growing out of control, and if left unchecked, they might just throw a party that I can't survive.

It's like having that uninvited guest who crashes on your couch and refuses to leave. Not exactly a smart move, given that this squatter seems intent on kicking me out of my own home! You'd think they'd show a little appreciation for the warm accommodation, but no, my squatter's ultimate game plan is to evict me from my own life. Well, I'm not having that!

The lead up, GPs, symptoms.

There are times in life when silence is not an option; when you must summon the courage to stand up and demand to be heard, even if it feels like you're shouting into a void. Nobody knows your body as intimately as you do. So, when something feels off, when the familiar rhythms of your health become disrupted, it is crucial to trust that instinct and advocate for yourself. This was my experience, and it marked the beginning of an arduous journey that would forever change my life.

It was a seemingly ordinary Wednesday afternoon in October, the sun casting a gentle light through the kitchen window. At 4:30 PM, I made the familiar trip from my home office to the kitchen, opening the fridge with the same casual ease that I had grown accustomed to in my routine. I pulled out a piece of ham, a staple of my new Slimming World diet. I had taken pride in my commitment to healthier eating, celebrating the small victories of weight loss and renewed vitality. Fruit and ham had become my go-to snacks, simple, satisfying, and low in calories.

But this day was different. As I took a bite of the ham, an unsettling sensation washed over me; it felt like it had lodged itself in my food pipe. My stomach dropped as confusion set in. What was happening? Had I rushed it? Had I failed to chew properly? Or was it something more insidious? Deep down, a voice whispered that this was not merely poor table manners gone awry.

I began to cough, hoping to dislodge the stubborn morsel, but my efforts were in vain. The urgent pressure in my chest grew worse, and I dashed to the bathroom, the walls closing in as panic started to creep into my mind. I wrenched my body, desperately trying to bring it back up, but nothing would move. After what felt like an eternity, around twenty minutes later, I managed to expel the food. My throat burned, and I gasped for relief. Yet, when I tentatively took a sip of water to wash away the bitter taste lingering in my mouth, my heart sank further, this too became stuck. In that moment, I realised the scope of my predicament was far beyond something as simple as eating too quickly.

Following the incident, I picked up the phone and called my GP's office, explaining my urgent need to be seen as soon as possible. The receptionist, however, became my first barrier. Despite my insistence, I could not shake the feeling that I was being dismissed. "If you're that worried, maybe you should go to Accident and Emergency," she suggested, a tone of indifference cloaked in her words. I hesitated. I knew too well how overwhelmed A&E could be; the idea of waiting for hours to simply be looked at made my stomach churn again.

Instead, I opted for the local out-of-hours walk-in centre. After enduring a lengthy wait, I finally found myself in front of a locum GP. My hope quickly dimmed as she treated my situation with apathy, making me feel like a burdensome inconvenience. It was as if I was merely a statistic in a busy clinic, not a person grappling with deep fears.

And then, as I watched her scribble notes without really engaging with me, I felt a surge of determination. I stopped her mid-sentence and locked eyes with her. "Are you okay?" I asked, my voice steady yet filled with earnest concern. The question hung in the air, the shock on her face was unmistakable. I pressed on, "You look like you're having some trouble listening to what I'm saying, and I feel like I'm in the way, is there something I can do for you?"

For the first time, she paused, the façade of disinterest cracking. Her attentiveness cracked through, and I took the opportunity to pour out my anxieties. I laid out everything: my recent episode, my family history of cancers, the alarming weight loss that I initially attributed to dieting success but now felt dreadfully significant.

By the time we reached seven o'clock, after a thorough recounting of my symptoms, the locum GP reluctantly suggested a two-week urgent cancer referral for an endoscopy. Though she seemed unconvinced it was serious, I felt a flicker of hope. This was progress. She wrote a note to my regular GP, and I left, fatigue weighing heavily on me, but a tentative sense of purpose building.

The following day, when I called my GP's office, I could never have expected the frustrating battle that lay ahead. After reviewing the locum's note, he expressed scepticism, maintaining that my symptoms were likely due to dysphagia, an issue he felt could be managed with medication. Time froze when I heard those words. "But" I insisted, "how is it acceptable to brush off my swallowing difficulties, my family history, and the weight loss as nothing to worry about?" I felt the urgency of my situation wrack my nerves as I pressed him further.

His assurance that I was too young for cancer echoed hollowly in my ears. "If only that were true," I murmured under my breath. Digging deep, I asserted myself, demanding he provide evidence to support his offhand diagnosis. It was only after my relentless persistence that he finally relented, agreeing to a referral.

I will carry that conversation with me for the rest of my life. Eloquent in its banality, it was also the catalyst of my survival, a lesson that unwavering self-advocacy can be a lifeline, particularly in moments when the stakes are immeasurably high. I had taken the first step into a labyrinth of uncertainty and fear, but I had learned an invaluable lesson: that voicing your truth can make all the difference.

Endoscopy, the day..."it's not good" & "That's a bit Shite!"

We all have those pivotal moments in our lives that shape who we are; birthdays, anniversaries, the first day on a new job, or the exciting start of university. But there are also moments that shatter our world, like the death of a loved one, or the day you find out you have cancer. I never thought I would find myself in such a devastating situation. Even as I underwent an endoscopy on the two-week cancer pathway, I thought that the doctor would simply tell me to lose weight, drink less, or that I had a stomach ulcer. But what I heard was far from any of that.

In movies, the scene often unfolds in a typical doctor's office, a clinical, sterile space. The doctor leans in, delivering the crushing news in a soft, gentle voice: "I'm sorry to tell you that you have cancer." The person receiving the news always has their significant other by their side, who comforts them with a reassuring hug, whispering that everything will be okay. The doctor adds, "Don't worry, we caught it early, and we can cure you." But my reality was distinctly different.

As I lay on the table during the endoscopy, I could hear the medical team talking in muted tones, phrases like "we'll take another" and "try a different angle" echoing in my ears. A nurse at my head gently stroked my hair and encouraged me, saying I was doing great and that it would be over soon. When the camera was finally withdrawn, the endoscopist approached, her eyes visible above her mask, and delivered the gut-wrenching phrase: "It's not good news." My immediate response was a stunned, "That's a bit shite!"

The moment set like stone in my mind, forever etched in my memory. I recall every detail. The temperature of the room, a chill brushing my skin, too warm to be termed "cold" yet enough to send shivers down my spine, the clatter of metal instruments collected into trays, the soft murmur of the nursing staff, the dim lighting that seemed to deepen the shadows of my despair, and the look in the clinician's eyes that shattered my world with four crushing words.

I was wheeled into the recovery area, a room divided into individual bays where some patients were recovering, laughing and joking with one another. The nurse placed me at the far end of the room, away from the others, and asked a colleague to keep an eye on me, understanding I had just received terrible news.

Sitting alone on the trolley bed, I felt utterly lost, grappling with a swirl of questions that raged in my mind like a tsunami: What happens now? How do I break this news to my husband, my children, my family and friends? What about my work? How long do I have left to live? Will I undergo treatment? Is this even treatable? The anxiety engulfed me, an overwhelming flood that threatened to drown my rationale.

After a seemingly endless stretch of time, the endoscopist returned and informed me she was arranging a CT scan, promising an update soon. She inquired if anyone was with me. I told her that my dad was waiting outside, having come to give me a ride home, just in case I needed sedation. I handed the nurse his number, and she called him to come to the recovery room.

When my dad arrived, the endoscopist motioned for him to join us in her office. As we walked through the corridor to that room, a stark space with a desk, an examination bed, and a few chairs, I felt a whirlwind of emotions.

She began explaining what they had discovered, but her words felt muddled, as if I were hearing them underwater. I understood the terminology, yet the gravity of it didn't register. I learned they had found a tumour located at the junction of my oesophagus and stomach. The endoscopist explained the challenges they faced in navigating the camera due to its location, but they managed to collect multiple biopsies to be tested for malignancy. When I asked for the likelihood of them being benign, she replied, "About 1%." I've always found solace in statistics, but in this case, it felt ominously clear: a 99% chance it was malignant. Just like that, I hadn't heard the word "cancer," yet I had already understood my fate.

She informed me that I would return on Monday for the CT scan, handed me some literature, and provided a nurse's contact information before we left.

As dad and I walked through the small garden back to the car park, I looked at him like I did when I was a child, desperately hoping he could somehow, miraculously, make everything right again. I realised, however, that wasn't going to happen. But in that moment, a resolution formed within me, I would be as strong as I could, taking each day and each challenge as it came. On the drive home, we talked about what would lay ahead, the statistics, the potential outcomes, and I steeled myself for a battle I never wanted but now had no choice but to face.

My Nurse Wendy.

I've always prided myself on my organisational skills. My work calendar is a well-crafted mosaic of events, projects, appointments, meetings, and important reminders. I thrive on structure, even to the point of obsession.

After my endoscopy, I was handed the name and number of a nurse, Wendy. When I returned home from my CT scan, I glanced at the scrawled name and telephone number, feeling a little confused. For the life of me, I couldn't remember why I had her contact information. Hesitating only for a moment, I picked up the phone and called.

"Hello, this is Wendy," a warm voice answered on the other end. I introduced myself, and to my surprise, she greeted me as if we were old friends. "I've been expecting your call," she said, with an assurance that instantly put me at ease.

As I stumbled through my uncertainty, Wendy patiently explained her role. She was there to co-ordinate all of my appointments and calls, to bridge the gaps among the four hospitals where my scans and potential treatments would take place. It was a relief to know that someone was managing this complex web of care on my behalf, although at this point, I had no real understanding of just how important this person would be to be.

Having spent nearly two decades working with NHS organisations, I understood how care pathways could become tangled between different providers. Each treatment and scan often needed a careful alignment of resources and schedules. But I had never truly grasped the logistical dance that went with my healthcare journey...until now.

As appointments began to flood in, with the intricate timelines demanding that MDTs reviewed results before further scans could be scheduled, I became aware of just important Wendy was in my treatment. Her presence made the daunting process feel steerable. She was not just a voice on the phone; she was a lifeline in a chaotic sea of medical uncertainties.

It struck me just how fortunate I was to have someone like Wendy in my corner. Many patients bravely walking a similar path might not have the same support. Understanding what scans were needed, the timeline for results, and how they all interlinked with each stage of treatment is crucial. Wendy helped me see that clarity and coordination are key to making this journey manageable.

As I hung up the phone after that first call, I couldn't help but feel a flicker of hope. With Wendy guiding me, perhaps I wouldn't just be surviving this journey; I could navigate it with a sense of purpose.

Biopsy results.

Waiting is part of the game, or at least that's what I kept telling myself to stay sane. But this wait, the wait for my biopsy results, felt like a cruel kind of limbo. A slow, stretched-out silence that echoed louder than any diagnosis ever could.

Rationally, I knew what the answer would be. Even before they scraped cells from my oesophagus and sent them off for analysis, even before the doctor tilted her head and said, "We'll need to confirm," I knew. Maybe not with 100% certainty, but close enough, 99% is a number that sticks in your head. I'd read the probabilities, I'd seen the scan, and I'd watched the expressions of medical professionals trained not to react. Still, there's a canyon between knowing and knowing. And until that phone rang, I was suspended somewhere in the middle.

I told my team I didn't want to wait for an appointment to hear my results. What's the point? I didn't need to get dressed up, drive to the hospital, navigate the impossible parking, and sit in an overly warm waiting room just to be told what could be said over the phone. I didn't need the ritual of it. I needed facts. I needed answers.

And more than that, I needed to be in control of how I received them.

Now, I know other people find comfort in the face-to-face delivery of difficult news. A chance to process things with someone right there, to ask questions at once. But I've always been a reflector. The big questions don't come when I'm staring at a consultant. They come later, in the car, in the shower, at 3 a.m. So, I asked them to call me as soon as they knew. That became a rhythm I stuck to throughout my treatment. Test, scan, phone call. Then I'd take my time, gather my thoughts, and go into the next appointment prepared with real, thoughtful questions. For me, it was a way of reclaiming a little bit of control in a process that so often strips it away.

When the call finally came, I answered before the first ring finished. I could tell from the tone of the voice on the other end, not cold, but careful, that it was what we suspected. "Yes," she said. "It is cancer." No dramatic music. No long preamble. Just quiet confirmation.

And oddly, I didn't feel much in that moment. Not panic. Not despair. Not relief either. I'd already absorbed the emotional impact days earlier, when I let myself imagine what this would mean. This call didn't change the trajectory I'd already mentally committed to; it simply confirmed the path I was already walking. And weirdly, that helped. Knowing is better than not knowing. Certainty, even when it's bad news, gives you something to push against. I wish I could say that this was the last time I had to wait by the phone. It wasn't. Not even close. One thing no one prepares you for in cancer treatment is just how much of it is about waiting. You think it's about medicine, surgery, decisions, and it is. But wrapped around all of that is the waiting. Waiting in clinics. Waiting in imaging suites. Waiting for blood tests to come back, for MDT meetings to happen, for surgeons to have space on their calendars. And above all, waiting for the damn thing to be gone. Waiting becomes the background noise of your life. And you get good at pretending it's not there, at going about your day while that anxious clock ticks in the back of your mind. But it's always there. Always.

The biopsy was just the beginning.

Telling people "I HAVE CANCER!!!"

It wasn't until after my treatment ended that I fully grasped the bewildering reality of being tasked with sharing the news of my cancer diagnosis. A patient, me, left to break the news to my family, friends, and employer without the benefit of any official training or emotional support. Meanwhile, the healthcare professionals who delivered the news to me were equipped with training in compassion and sensitivity, as if the weight of such devastating words could somehow be made lighter through careful phrasing. Reflecting on it now, I realise that there should be some kind of guidance for the ones who find themselves in our shoes, forced to relay heavy news without a roadmap. While I understand that a formal program might not be possible, the act of informing loved ones about my cancer was filled with complexity, and I often feel compelled to apologise to the first few people I confided in.

The very first time I uttered the phrase "I HAVE CANCER!!!!!" it shot out of my mouth like a cannon, loaded with raw emotion and fear, yet lacking any forethought about how it would land on the ears of others. The silence that followed felt like a lead balloon dropping into a deep ocean, creating ripples of shock and disbelief. Their reactions were telling. "What?" "Say again... you have what?" The disbelief lingered in the air, almost palpable, as I tried to clarify what I had just said. With every subsequent conversation, I learned the importance of easing into the announcement, careful to prep my audience for the gravity of what I was about to share.

"I have some not-so-great news to share with you," or "This isn't going to be an easy conversation" became my warm-up phrases, akin to a coach preparing their team for the challenging game ahead. I would paint the story of my diagnosis in broad strokes, often narrowing it into specific moments that evoked both vulnerability and honesty, but ultimately led to an ending that was, at that point, still uncertain. The gradual build-up gave my friends and family a moment to brace themselves for the truth, turning what could have been a sudden emotional blast into a more manageable wave.

For the most part, the responses were predictably tender. A hush would settle over the room, occasionally interrupted by the brief sound of a sob or the dull thud of a heart sinking. The expected phrases would follow, all poured forth from genuine love: "You'll be fine." "They can do marvellous things these days." "More people survive cancer than ever now." While these sentiments were well-intentioned, they didn't always resonate with me. They felt like a life preserver thrown into turbulent waters, well-meaning but insufficient against the chaos swirling in my mind, questions of uncertainty gnawed at me: "What if it's not okay?" "What if the treatment doesn't work?" "What if I'm not one of the survivors?"

Their heartfelt inquiries about my treatment plan only added to my internal conflict. In those first moments, I grappled with an overwhelming mix of new information, fear, and a façade of composure that crumbled under the weight of my anxiety. I found myself in an uncomfortable position, peeling back layers of my situation while trying to navigate the raw emotions and fragility both they and I felt in that space.

Then there was the inevitable cycle of updates. Sharing my journey wasn't merely a one-time announcement but became an ongoing narrative, a repetitive musical refrain that dominated our conversations. Each time I had to deliver the news, it felt like putting on the same heavy coat, each detail carrying both the weight of my reality and the expectations of concern from those who cared about me.

In the end, sharing my cancer journey became a series of lessons, not just about the body and illness, but about the intricacies of human patterns and relationships. Yes, there were difficulties and losses, but there were also moments of unexpected kindness, connection, and, most importantly, an understanding that even in the bleakest circumstances, the human heart is capable of tremendous resilience. Even in the darkest of times, I learned to navigate this new reality with grace, approaching each conversation as a human touchpoint; a bridge built from vulnerability, honesty, and an extensive amount of love, both given and received.

GULP

David Jones-Stanley

Part 3
Navigating the
Experience

"I wasn't just another patient;
I was a participant, ready to engage
in conversations that would shape
my future."

GULP

Learn, Learn, Learn.

In the late '90s, former British Prime Minister Tony Blair famously declared, "Education, Education, Education!", a catchy mantra intended to steer a nation through a pivotal moment in history.

Now, I may not be a politician, and truthfully, I'm quite thankful for that, can you imagine the endless debates? Who has that kind of time? However, I've always believed that education forms the cornerstone of understanding the world around us. The more informed we are, the better equipped we are to handle life's challenges, especially the monumental struggles such as facing a serious illness.

When I received my cancer diagnosis, a dear friend offered me a thoughtful gift that changed everything, "The Streetwise Guide to Surviving Cancer". Spoiler alert: it's a fantastic read! This book was not just a gift; it was an invitation; a door opened to a journey I never anticipated embarking on. I suddenly found myself on a quest, propelled by an insatiable need to learn everything I could about my unwelcome squatter, a.k.a. my cancer. What was it? How did it sneak in uninvited? What treatments might send it packing for good?

As I delved deeper into the world of cancer, I was hit with a brutal reality check. This squatter had the potential to wreak havoc in ways I could scarcely imagine, and the survival rates were grim. But amidst the overwhelming statistics and dire predictions, I discovered something transformative: knowledge was my ticket to empowerment. In a universe that often felt chaotic and entirely out of my control, gaining insight into my cancer provided me with the ability to navigate the turbulent waters of uncertainty and reclaim a little agency over my own situation.

The moment I was diagnosed with oesophageal cancer marked a significant shift in my life. Yet, this experience spiralled into a second journey: a profound and intricate quest for knowledge. I recognised the profound truth in the idea that knowledge could empower me. I truly believed that the more I could understand the complexities and realities of my condition, the better I would be at charting my path through the daunting waters ahead.

This thirst for knowledge wasn't an entirely new concept for me. Throughout my youth, I had an insatiable curiosity, an inherent drive to dissect and analyse everything in my environment. I would spend countless hours taking apart my favourite toys, driven by an innate desire to discover the mechanics hidden within each piece. My fascination with how things worked extended beyond playtime; it grew into a deep love for educational content, particularly television programs that unravelled the intricacies of engineering and innovation. I revelled in these learning moments, and even today, I often find myself glued to the screen watching documentaries with my children, exploring the various wonders of the world together. My passion for learning didn't stop there; I still eagerly immerse myself in Lego manuals with a level of enthusiasm that might seem unusual for my age! Truly, I have always been hardwired for curiosity.

As I transitioned into adulthood, I channelled this love for exploration into a career dedicated to understanding complex systems. My professional life revolved around grasping the "whys" and "how's" of the world. In my field, knowledge truly is power, and this philosophy became my steadfast companion during the difficult trials of my cancer journey. It offered me a sense of solace and direction amidst chaos.

When I immersed myself in information about oesophageal cancer, I made a surprising discovery: despite my daunting diagnosis, I was fortunate. It felt oddly unsettling to label myself as "lucky" when confronted by such a fearsome adversary as cancer. Yet, the statistics provided a glimmer of clarity, if not hope, which I often hesitate to embrace. In the UK, roughly one-third of patients diagnosed with oesophageal cancer are granted a chance at a curative pathway; the remaining two-thirds face a grim reality of palliative care. This stark realisation propelled me to dig deeper into the disease. I learned that oesophageal cancer often presents at advanced stages, with symptoms that are easily overlooked or misinterpreted for long periods.

Through diligent research and meaningful discussions, the gravity of the survival rates dawned on me. Despite this heaviness, my desire for knowledge only intensified. It felt akin to watching a horror film with my hands partially covering my eyes; I was both terrified and drawn in with an irrepressible urge to understand the shadows lurking around my situation. My pivotal consultation with an oncologist came swiftly, just a day after my diagnosis, and it marked the beginning of a crucial phase in my journey.

With this meeting, I began to familiarise myself with an array of treatment options: chemoradiotherapy, chemotherapy, surgical interventions, and various combinations of these strategies. Armed with the knowledge I had gained through my readings, I felt empowered. I wasn't just another patient; I was a participant, ready to engage in conversations that would shape my future. When I met my oncology team a few days later, I arrived fully prepared, with a mind buzzing with inquiries, insights, and a clearer understanding of what lay ahead.

The difference this preparation made was staggering. In my exchanges with my oncology team, the dynamic shifted significantly compared to experiences I'd had with other healthcare professionals. Because I had done my homework, they didn't need to spend time explaining the basics. I was no longer a passive recipient of information; I had transformed into an active participant in my own healthcare journey. Our discussions were richer, filled with depth and detail, and I experienced a renewed sense of agency over my treatment options. No longer did I feel like a victim of fate or fear; I stood firm and equipped with knowledge, and more importantly, the confidence that went with it.

This transformation from a passive patient to an informed participant marked a significant turning point in my journey. Armed with knowledge, I was poised to make informed choices about my treatment while advocating for my own needs. This newfound sense of empowerment fortified my resolve, turning what could have been a path riddled with anxiety into a meaningful exploration of my health. And this was just the beginning. As I moved forward, navigating the complexities of my diagnosis, I vowed to continue sharing this philosophy, not only with myself but also with others enduring similar battles. Because in an unpredictable world, knowledge appears not simply as a shield but a powerful ally.

One word of caution, though: while curiosity and research are invaluable, not all information is created equal. In the age of the internet, it can be tempting to Google every symptom or latch onto alarming stories from questionable sources. I quickly learned how misleading and even dangerous that approach can be. Instead, rely on reputable, trustworthy websites.

Navigating the system.

The NHS. A blessing, no doubt. But when you're suddenly thrust into it as a cancer patient, it can feel less like a lifeline and more like a labyrinth. It's a system full of brilliant people working in impossible conditions, and yet, as a patient, especially a newly diagnosed one, it's incredibly easy to feel lost.

I didn't know the first thing about how cancer care worked when I started. I had this vague idea that once you were diagnosed, things would just happen. Like there was a conveyor belt and you'd be placed on it, gently and efficiently rolled through all the right scans, meetings, treatments, and follow-ups. But that's not quite how it goes.

Here's what I learned.

First, no one is coming to hold your hand. That sounds harsh, but it's true. You will meet some incredible, kind professionals, nurses, consultants, co-ordinators, but the truth is, you have to advocate for yourself. You have to ask questions, chase appointments, follow up on test results. The system is overstretched, and things can fall through the cracks. So as much as you might feel like retreating inward, and believe me,

I did, you also need to be your own project manager.

I kept a notebook from day one. Names of consultants. Dates of tests. Questions I had. Answers I didn't fully understand. If I'd waited until I was sitting in front of someone to remember what I wanted to ask, I'd have forgotten everything. Cancer brain is real, and fear scrambles your memory like nothing else. Writing things down saved me time, energy, and sanity.

Appointments can be confusing. One day you're in a local hospital for a CT scan, the next you're in a specialist centre seeing someone whose title you don't even fully understand. You start collecting departments like Pokémon cards, ENT, oncology, gastroenterology, radiology, surgery, and it's not always clear who's in charge. Spoiler: you are. Or at least, you have to behave like you are. Because while there is usually a "lead consultant" or a "clinical nurse specialist" (CNS) co-ordinating your case, you'll often be the only person who sees the full picture.

One of the more frustrating things is communication between departments. I'd get a scan in one place, then weeks later find out the results hadn't made it to the right team. Or someone would say, "Oh, you haven't had that test yet?" and I'd think, wasn't that your job to know? It's not about blame, it's about bandwidth. Everyone's juggling too much, and sometimes, you just have to be politely persistent.

So here are some tips, from one patient to another:

1. Get a notebook or use your phone. Write down every appointment, question, result, and conversation. It becomes your Cancer Bible.

2. Learn names and roles. Knowing who does what helps you direct questions properly. Don't be afraid to ask, what exactly is your role in my care?

3. Chase things. If you're waiting on a result and haven't heard back in a week or two, call. Your CNS or cancer co-ordinator is usually the best first point of contact.

4. Bring someone with you. If you can. Another pair of ears makes a huge difference. Or ask if you can record your consultations, most doctors are fine with it if you ask politely.

5. Don't be afraid to be 'that' patient. You're not being difficult. You're being thorough. This is your life we're talking about.

One thing I do want to say, through all of this, I never lost respect for the people working in the

NHS. They were under pressure, overworked, and still found time to look me in the eye and ask how I was. It's not a perfect system, but it's a human one. That means it needs patients to be human too, vulnerable, yes, but also proactive.

Cancer already takes so much out of you. Navigating the system shouldn't be one more thing that breaks you down. So, take control where you can. Ask questions. Speak-up. Write it down. Follow-up. And when the system stumbles, because sometimes it will, don't take it personally.

Just get back on the phone and keep going.

Because the NHS is big, yes. And complex. But it's also made up of people who genuinely want to help you get through this. Sometimes, they just need a little help helping you.

Ask questions.
(even if they don't like it!)

If cancer teaches you anything early on, it's that you have to show up for yourself, fully. No one else is going to do it for you. That's not a criticism of the system or the people within it, I met some incredible doctors, nurses, and specialists along the way. But they're dealing with hundreds, even thousands, of patients. You're dealing with one. You. And you can't afford to sit quietly in the back seat of your own treatment plan. You have to get in the front, "hands on" the wheel.

At the start, I didn't ask many questions. I didn't want to be a nuisance or seem like I didn't trust the experts. I nodded through consultations, pretended to understand things I didn't, and left rooms with more questions than answers. I was scared, overwhelmed, and trying to keep up with something that had completely overtaken my life. It felt like I was being carried along by a current I couldn't fight.

But then came a turning point, I remember sitting in one consultation, completely lost in the flood of medical jargon. They were talking about scan results, staging, treatment options. I was nodding, but inside, I was panicking. I had no idea what any of it really meant. Finally, I interrupted and said, "Sorry, can you explain that in plain English?" And just like that, the whole atmosphere changed. The conversation slowed down. I could breathe again. I wasn't just a name on a chart. I was a person trying to understand what the hell was happening to him.

That one moment shifted everything for me. From then on, I decided I would always ask the questions I needed to ask, no matter how obvious or awkward they might seem. I wasn't trying to be difficult. I was trying to stay involved, to understand my own care, and to make decisions with confidence. This wasn't just happening to me, I was part of it.

Of course, speaking up doesn't always come easy. Sometimes you'll meet resistance, a consultant who's in a rush, a nurse who doesn't have the full picture, or a process that just doesn't leave room for your voice. But even when it feels uncomfortable, even when you think you're being a pain, you have to say something. Ask again. Slow things down. Say, "I'm not sure I understand." That's not weakness, that's strength.

Before appointments, I started writing down questions on my phone. Things I thought of in the shower, lying awake at night, or even mid-way through watching TV. It sounds simple, but it meant I never sat in those rooms feeling like I had forgotten the one thing I really wanted to ask. And I stopped being afraid to repeat myself. Sometimes I'd say, "I know we talked about this before, but can you go over it again?" The good ones never minded. And if someone did mind? Well, that told me something too.

When I could, I brought someone with me. A second pair of ears helps more than you'd think. Even just having someone to debrief with afterwards made a difference. So many times, I'd say, "Did he really say that?" and they'd say, "Yes, and he also said this," and I'd realise how much I'd missed in the fog of it all.

But the biggest shift was internal. I stopped seeing myself as a passive patient and started behaving like a partner in my own care. That doesn't mean I suddenly had all the answers. It just meant I gave myself permission to be there, fully and actively. To ask. To question. To understand. And, at times, to challenge.

That's the heart of this chapter. You have the right, and the responsibility, to speak-up. This is your body. Your life. Your treatment. You're allowed to take up space in that consultation room. You're allowed to need more time. You're allowed to want clarity. You're allowed to say, "This doesn't feel right." That's not being difficult. That's being invested.

And when you find the courage to do that, to advocate for yourself, things begin to shift. Not always dramatically, not always instantly. But you start to feel more in control, even when everything around you feel uncertain.

So don't sit quietly and hope it all makes sense later. Ask now. Speak now. Be your own advocate, because you know yourself better than anyone else possibly could.

And if your voice shakes when you do it, let it shake. But use it anyway.

You're in control, it's your decision...your body...your journey.

Control. It's a funny concept, isn't it? We talk about it all the time. Taking control. Staying in control. Regaining control. But when you're diagnosed with something like cancer, you realise just how slippery that word really is. People tell you to take charge of your journey, but how do you do that when something inside your own body is misbehaving? When there's a tumour growing, silent and stubborn, with no regard for your timetable, your plans, your life?

The doctors can't always say how fast it's growing, or even how it behaves. Is it aggressive? Dormant? Somewhere in between? And so, you're left with this surreal situation. You're being told to take control, but your body seems to be operating on its own terms. That disconnect, between what you're told and what you feel, is disorienting. It rattles you.

I found that especially hard at the start. Not knowing what treatment, I would get. Not knowing whether I'd have any say in the matter. It felt like I'd been thrown into a fast-moving river without a paddle. You assume you'll be asked what's best for you. That your life, your routines, your ability to cope, will be taken into consideration. You assume there will be room for a conversation.

Sometimes, there isn't.

When you first sit down with the clinical team, they often present a plan like it's already been carved into stone. A pre-set path. One-size-fits all. There's a quiet assumption in the room: "We've seen this before. We know what to do." And yes, they've seen people with similar symptoms. People with similar scans. People with similar demographics, similar tumour locations, similar disease progression.

But here's the truth I had to learn, the truth I hope you never forget. You are not just a case file. You are not just a diagnosis. You are not just the latest person to sit in that chair.

You are you. Entirely and unapologetically you. And that matters.

I remember a particular meeting with one of the oncologists. She came in briskly, spoke with authority, laid out the plan. Chemotherapy. These drugs. These dates. This side effect profile. This schedule. She talked at me, not with me. There was no question of whether I agreed or whether I had preferences, whether there might be other paths to explore. Just: this is what we're doing.

And I remember stopping her. I asked why I wasn't being offered another treatment that I'd read about. I knew it had recently been approved for my specific tumour type. I wasn't trying to be difficult. I wasn't rejecting the plan. I just wanted to understand. I wanted to have a voice.

The response? A flat statement. "That's not available for your condition."

Except, I knew it was. The approval had come through just the week before. I'd done my research. So, I pressed again. She hesitated. And then, realising I might be right, she left the room and speak to someone else. She had to check.

That moment was a revelation for me. A quiet but powerful realisation. Doctors do not know everything. They're experts, yes. They're trained, yes. But they are not infallible. And most importantly, they do not know you the way you know yourself.

From that point forward I started to push for real discussions. I didn't want instructions. I wanted conversations. I wanted options on the table, with the pros and cons laid out in full. I wanted to understand. Not just to be told, but to be informed. To be respected as a person, not just managed as a patient.

Because control, real control, doesn't mean dictating the entire course of your treatment. It doesn't mean ignoring the professionals or thinking you know more than they do. It means being involved. It means showing up with curiosity, asking the difficult questions, trusting your instincts, and insisting on being heard.

It means recognising that while clinicians are experts in medicine, you are the expert in your own life.

The more I understood what was happening to me, the better I could cope. The more I asked, the more I learned, the more I realised that knowledge wasn't just power, it was peace. When you know why you're doing something, when you understand the purpose and the science behind it, it stops being something done to you and becomes something your part of.

Without that understanding, it's easy to feel like a bystander in your own story. Like you're just being carried along by a current you can't fight. But you're not a passenger. You're the main character. The protagonist. The one whose body and soul are going through this.

And once you grasp that, everything starts to shift.

The clinicians may walk into the room with their degrees and protocols, and that's fine. But don't let their confidence silence your voice. Don't forget that you are the most important person in any room where your care is being discussed.

That's not arrogance. That's fact.

Control comes from awareness. From education. From engagement. It comes from refusing to be reduced to a number on a chart. And yes, there will be days when you're tired, overwhelmed, and just want someone else to make the decisions. That's okay too. But when you can, when you have the strength, take your seat at the table.

You are not just surviving cancer. You are participating in your healing.

That, in the end, is what control really means.

GULP

Part 4
Emotional and Psychological Aspects

"This situation is terrible, but we're still here. We're still us."

Don't ask, don't tell.

Navigating conversations after a cancer diagnosis isn't as straightforward as people might think. It's not just about discussing symptoms with doctors or checking in with family. In those spaces, talking about cancer is expected, sometimes it's all you can talk about. But outside that inner circle, in everyday life, things get murky.

I'm talking about chats with friends, acquaintances, work colleagues, the window cleaner, the checkout assistant at the supermarket. These aren't people you sit down with and pour your heart out to, but they're people you still interact with. Often, they "know". Or at least suspect. And you know they know. It becomes this quiet dance of assumption and avoidance.

There's this odd moment of recognition. Maybe they're wondering why you look different or maybe it's the hair loss, the pale skin, the weight change, or just the general "unwell" look that can linger. For men, it can be more subtle. Baldness is common, but take away eyebrows and eyelashes, and there's a different kind of visibility. A wordless acknowledgment hangs in the air...but no one dare name it.

Sometimes, I do want to talk about it. I want to crack through the awkwardness, to take control of the narrative instead of leaving people to guess. I want to say, "Yes, I'm having treatment. Yes, it's hard. But I'm here, and I'm still me."

But other times? I want to pretend nothing's wrong.

I want a moment of normal.

There was this one day, I was out shopping, just ticking things off a list, hoping to be in and out quickly. I ran into an old neighbour. They'd moved away about a year before my diagnosis, so they had no idea what I'd been going through. We stood in the middle of the aisle, surrounded by signs screaming "Buy One Get One Free!" and we chatted. They asked about the kids, how work was going, if the local bakery still did those sausage rolls they liked. I could feel it in their eyes, that hesitation, that wondering. Do I ask? Do I say something?

I could've told them. But I didn't.

In that moment, I wasn't cancer. I was just a person shopping, reconnecting, engaging in small talk like nothing had changed. I even caught myself rubbing my chin, an old habit from when I had a beard. There was no beard now, of course. Just muscle memory. A nod to who I used to be.

And you know what? It felt good.

I walked away from that encounter with a strange sense of peace. I realised something important: not everyone has the right to know. Not everyone needs to know.

This is my story.

I get to choose who I tell, when I tell them, and how I tell it...if I tell it at all.

That's something cancer doesn't get to take from me: my voice, my privacy, my boundaries.

But the opposite is also true. There are moments when I need to talk. Not want, need. Moments when the weight of it all presses so heavily on my chest that if I don't speak, I might suffocate. The silence becomes too loud. Those are the hardest conversations, not because others bring them up, but because they don't.

I've learned that some people don't want to hear it. Not because they don't care, but because they're scared. They don't know what to say, so they say nothing at all. They change the subject. They fidget. They deflect with jokes. They mean well, but the silence feels like rejection.

David Jones-Stanley

In those moments, I have to decide what matters more: their comfort or my truth?

I've learned that my truth matters.

I matter.

What I feel, what I carry, what I need to release, it's not a burden. It's not an inconvenience. It's real. And if someone isn't ready to hear it, that's okay. But I no longer swallow my words to make others more comfortable. The silence I keep now is chosen, not forced.

Cancer taught me a lot of things, many of them unwanted lessons. But one thing I've come to truly understand is this: my story is mine. And in a world that often asks us to perform our pain for others, it's an act of power to choose when to speak, and when to stay silent.

So, if you ever find yourself wondering whether you should ask me about my cancer, the answer is: it depends. Not on you, but on me.

Some days I'll want to tell you everything.

Other days, I'll just want to talk about the weather or the price of strawberries.

And both are valid.

GULP

Dear friends.

Here's the thing no one really wants to tell you. You will lose friends along this journey. There, I said it.

It's not a warning, not a bitter statement, and certainly not something I say lightly. It's just the truth. A quiet, uncomfortable truth that many people living with cancer eventually discover. When I was first diagnosed, no one mentioned it. No doctor, no leaflet, no survivor blog or support group hinted at it. And yet, it unfolded just as surely as the hair loss, the appointments, the scanxiety.

Slowly, quietly, painfully, I lost people I thought I would never lose.

To be fair, I've never been someone surrounded by a massive circle of die-hard friends I know a lot of people. I have an extended family that's both sprawling and loving in its own chaotic way. I have acquaintances, colleagues, neighbours. But my real friends, the kind I let in, the kind who know where the light switches are in my house without asking, are few. Carefully chosen. Deep connections rather than wide ones. And then, within that small circle, I have what I call my dear friends. These are the ones who know all of it. The ones who text at 2 a.m. because they just had a feeling. The ones who held me when I cried and didn't try to fix anything, because they knew they couldn't.

These are the people I turned to first. The ones I blurted out "I HAVE CANCER" to, barely able to say the words. The ones who sat in silence when silence was what I needed, who didn't flinch when I talked about death or fear or how exhausted I was from pretending I was okay. The ones who never made it about them. These people did not run. These people stayed. And I love them more fiercely now than I ever did before.

But then there were the others.

The almost-friends. The people on the periphery. The ones who might've made it into the inner circle one day. People I used to grab coffee with, message memes to share good news and stupid complaints with. People who, before all of this, felt like future lifelong friends. And I lost them.

At first, it's subtle. A delayed reply. A missed call. A string of well-meaning texts that eventually dry up. The invitations that stop coming. And then it becomes more obvious, they go quiet. Vanish.

Disappear from your life like a puff of smoke. Some people just couldn't be around my illness. Not because they didn't care, but because they didn't know how to care. Because cancer doesn't just challenge the person who has it, it exposes the people around them too.

And here's the uncomfortable part:

I understand it.

I really do.

Cancer is messy and frightening. It strips away the illusion of control. It reminds you that bodies break, that lives are fragile, that everything can change with one phone call. Not everyone can sit with that reality. Some people look at you and see their own worst fears reflected back at them. And I can't be angry at them for that.

In fact, if I'm honest, if there had been a way for me to run from it, I probably would have too. If I could have handed my body and my diagnosis to someone else and walked away with clean hands and no scars, I'd have done it in a heartbeat.

But I couldn't. And I didn't have the luxury of disappearing. They did.

What surprised me most wasn't their silence it was the performance of presence. The social media likes. The "You've got this!" comments. The fist bump emojis and "thinking of you hun xx" messages. The bright and breezy declarations of support that showed up in public, but never in private. I became fluent in that language. The language of performative encouragement. And while part of me appreciated it, because at least they didn't say the wrong thing directly to my face, another part of me was quietly mourning the friendships that had dissolved beneath those cheery slogans.

"You've got this" doesn't carry the same weight when it's posted on your Facebook wall by someone who hasn't checked in for six months. When it comes from someone who never asked if you wanted company at your appointment, or if you had enough groceries in the fridge. It doesn't comfort you when you're crying into your pillow at 4 a.m., terrified that this thing inside your body is going to win.

Friendship, real friendship, isn't loud. It doesn't always show up on social media. Sometimes it's the quiet text that says, "No need to reply, just thinking of you." Sometimes it's someone dropping off a meal or sitting beside you on the sofa while you fall asleep halfway through a film. Sometimes it's just showing up, even when they don't know what to say.

Cancer shows you who those people are. And it also shows you who they're not.

I've lost friends in this process. But I've also learned what friendship truly means. I've learned that some people come with you, and some people can't. And that's okay. Not everyone is meant to walk the whole road with you. Some people are only there for a chapter. It doesn't make them bad it just makes them temporary.

So, if you're reading this and you're grieving the loss of friendships you thought were forever, know that you're not alone. It happens. It hurts. And it's part of this wild, unpredictable, sometimes unbearably beautiful thing we call survivorship.

The people who matter will stay.

The ones who disappear made space for the ones who truly belong.

And that, I think, is a kind of gift too.

A laugh a minute.

Laughter has always been my default setting. When things get too much, when emotions threaten to boil over, when I don't know whether to cry or scream, I laugh. It's not always intentional; it's just how I cope. I've laughed at funerals, giggled uncontrollably when nervous, and cracked one-liners in the middle of deeply awkward silences. Some people might see that as inappropriate, but for me, it's survival. Laughter is my pressure valve. And during my cancer journey, it became more important than ever.

Now, don't get me wrong, cancer is not funny. There's nothing humorous about being told you have a tumour growing in your oesophagus or waking up from surgery with tubes sticking out of you like some kind of sci-fi prop. But even in those moments, or especially in those moments, I looked for something to laugh about. I made it my mission: if I could find even one thing each day to smile or laugh at, then cancer wasn't winning. It could take my hair, my food pipe, even my stomach, but it was not taking my sense of humour. That was non-negotiable.

One of my favourite memories, one that still
makes me smile, is about my dad. He came with
me to almost every appointment, bless him. At 72,
he became my chauffeur, my sidekick, my
emotional anchor. And to be honest, he was doing
better than I was most days, fitter, more alert, and
somehow always dressed in clean clothes, which
was more than I could say for myself.

So, we'd be sitting in the hospital waiting room,
surrounded by other patients, many looking
understandably worn down by their own
journeys. And the nurse would come out, glance
around, and look straight at him.

"The Dr won't be long", she would say...to him.

I'd nudge him. "Dad, they think you have the
cancer. You really need to start looking less
healthy!" He'd laugh, I'd laugh, and the poor nurse
would usually blush and mumble something as
she walked away.

It became a running joke. We'd even come up
with imaginary ailments for him to 'pretend' to
have next time: "Tell them you've got athlete's foot
of the oesophagus," I'd whisper. He rolled his eyes
but played along.

Humour became our shared language. It
helped both of us cope, me with the pain, and him

with the helplessness of watching his child go through something so harrowing.

We'd crack jokes in the car, playfully argue over which waiting room had the worst TV programs and silently rate the hospital food like we were on MasterChef. It wasn't about pretending everything was fine. It was about saying, "This situation is terrible, but we're still here. We're still us."

Not everyone appreciated it. You'd get the occasional disapproving glare when you're sniggering in a cancer clinic waiting room. One lady once actually shushed us. I suppose in her mind, if you're laughing, you must not be suffering enough. But I've learned not to take that personally. Some people cry; others go quiet. I laugh. That's my way of processing the madness. And frankly, if anyone was allowed to laugh in that place, I figured it was me.

Of course, there were darker days. Days when nothing felt remotely funny. Days when I didn't want to get out of bed, let alone find the energy to crack a joke. And that's okay too. Humour doesn't erase the pain, but it does help you carry it. It lightens the load, even if just for a moment.

So, whether it's laughter, music, sarcasm, dance, drawing, or quietly mouthing off under your breath, find your coping mechanism. Hold it close. Guard it fiercely. Because you're going to need something to get you through the long hours, the long nights, the long waits, and the long silences.

Laughter, for me, wasn't just a reaction, it was resistance. It was my way of saying, "You can mess with my body, cancer, but you're not touching my spirit."

And on some days, when everything else felt out of control, that tiny giggle, shared with my dad, or even to myself, was enough to remind me: I'm still here.

Still fighting.

Still laughing.

Comedy helped.

In the previous chapter, I talked about how laughter became my coping mechanism, a reflex, a shield, a lifeline. But comedy did more than just help me survive, it became a way to connect. With others. With myself. With the messiness of it all. Because when you're staring down something as enormous as cancer, sometimes the only thing you can do is laugh.

And laugh I did.

One of my proudest achievements during treatment was discovering that "I have The Cancer" always with that dramatic emphasis, was the ultimate get-out-of-anything card.

Dishes?

"I can't possibly clean the dishes... I have The Cancer."

Shopping?

"Go to the shops? Me? With The Cancer? How dare you."

It became a running joke in my house. I'd pull it out anytime something dull or inconvenient came up. Need to walk the dog? "Oh no, not today. The Cancer." It was ridiculous, and I knew it, but

73

that was the point. If I was going to have cancer, I figured I might as well milk it for a few perks.

Now, don't get me wrong, laughter can be the best medicine. Unless it's cancer. Then chemo is much better.

But in between treatments, in waiting rooms, in the early hours of the morning when the world felt far away and nothing made sense, laughter helped. It wasn't a cure, but it was a tonic. A way to reclaim something light in the middle of it all.

My friends rolled their eyes. My family laughed. But more than that, it relieved people. It gave them permission to smile, to stop walking on eggshells, to talk to me like a normal person again instead of a porcelain doll wrapped in sympathy.

One afternoon, a mate popped over and offered to help around the house. I said, "Thanks, but unless you're offering to carry me dramatically up the stairs like a Victorian heroine, I'm good." He laughed so hard he forgot the awkward pep talk he'd clearly been preparing. We ended up talking about everything but cancer for two hours. Bliss.

What I didn't realise at first was how much this humour wasn't just for me it was for them too. Cancer makes people uncomfortable. It reminds them of their own vulnerability, of how fragile things are. But a giggle, a smile, even a poorly timed pun, suddenly made it okay to be around me. It broke the ice. It made space for honesty.

In fact, I lost count of the number of times someone would laugh at one of my ridiculous one-liners and then, in a quieter moment open up. They'd say, "My mum had cancer," or "I've been so scared to talk to you about it," or "I didn't know if I was allowed to laugh." And just like that, we'd be in a real conversation. One that mattered.

Even strangers got in on it. While waiting for an appointment, the receptionist asked how I was. I smiled sweetly and said, "Surviving, the poison hasn't killed me yet! Thanks for asking." She burst out laughing. It was silly, but for a moment, we were just two people sharing a joke, not a patient and a clipboard.

Humour was my way of saying: "Yes, this sucks. But I'm still here. I'm still me."

Of course, not everyone got it. There were those who thought joking about cancer was inappropriate or flippant. But what they didn't see were the dark days. The tears. The fear. The nights when I'd lie awake feeling like my body was turning against me. The jokes were never about pretending it was easy, they were about surviving it.

Comedy didn't cure anything. But it helped carry it. It made things just a little lighter. And in a world that had become heavy and unpredictable, that was everything.

So yes, I used humour to dodge housework. Yes, I played the Cancer Card like a pro. But I also used it to stay connected to the world, to remind myself that I wasn't just a patient, I was a person. A sarcastic, laughing, still here person.

And some days, when nothing else made sense, when the scans were bad or the pain was worse, a single joke, shared with a nurse, a friend, or just me, was enough to tip the scale. Enough to say, "You haven't taken this from me. Not today."

Cancer can, and does, take a lot. But it wasn't taking my spirit. And definitely not my punchlines.

Choosing your attitude.

You can be miserable, unpleasant and utterly foul, if that's what you want to be. And believe me, no one has the right to tell you that's not fair or valid. Cancer is a beast. If you want to cry, scream, hide under the duvet and tell the world to sod off then that's allowed.

But here's the thing. Cancer was happening to me whether I liked it or not. That part wasn't optional. The tumour in my oesophagus didn't give a toss about my mood. So, I had two choices: I could be angry, bitter, and still have cancer... or I could be kind, hopeful (on most days), and still have cancer. Either way, the cancer was staying. Everything else? That was mine to choose.

And I chose a positive attitude.

Now don't get me wrong I'm not here to tell anyone how to feel or how to behave. There's no manual for this kind of thing. Everyone's journey is different. But for me, choosing my attitude, again and again, every single day, changed how I lived with cancer.

Make no mistake, this wasn't about pretending everything was fine. It wasn't about toxic positivity or forcing a smile when I felt like screaming. It was about showing up anyway. Even when it was hard... Especially when it was hard.

There were mornings when I woke up and every bone in my body said, "Nope." Days when I wanted to stay in bed, skip the meds, avoid the food, and just check-out completely. And honestly, on some days, I did. I'm human. But most days, I got up. I washed. I ate something. I exercised, even just a slow walk to the kitchen. I took my pills. I spoke to people. I cracked a joke, if I had one in me. And I did all that not because I was full of joy and energy, but because I'd chosen not to let cancer decide everything.

Choosing to keep going, even in small ways, helped me feel like I still had some control. It gave shape to my days. It gave me strength, not the heroic kind, just the "I got through the morning" kind. And that was enough.

Humour, of course, was a huge part of that. As I've said before, I took the piss out of the situation whenever I could. Cancer gave me very few perks, but it did give me some decent material. If someone asked how I was doing, I'd say something like, "Oh you know, just enjoying the all-inclusive holiday at Chemo Spa, terrible food, but excellent service." It wasn't about making light of the illness. It was about refusing to be consumed by it.

What I found, surprisingly, was that when I kept a light touch, it helped other people too. It opened them up. They weren't so scared to talk to me. I wasn't just a sick person in their eyes, I was me, still sarcastic, still stubborn, still cracking jokes no matter what.

And there's something powerful about that. There's dignity in it. Not the quiet, noble kind you see in films, but the messy, real-life kind. The "I brushed my hair today and made my own cup of tea" kind. That's victory. That's strength.

Let's be real, though. Positivity didn't make the pain go away. It didn't stop the side effects. It didn't magically heal me. But it helped me cope. And coping, in my book, is a damn good achievement.

There were also days where the choice wasn't easy. Days when positivity felt fake. Days when my body hurt, my mind was foggy, and the whole "attitude is everything" idea made me want to punch a motivational speaker. On those days, I didn't aim for joy. I aimed for neutral. And even that was progress.

Here's what I've learned: Choosing Attitude Isn't about pretending. It's about responding. Life throws you things you didn't ask for, big, horrible, messy things. But you still get to choose how you meet them. Maybe not with grace, but with grit. With stubbornness. With humour. With a bit of middle-finger energy if needed.

And sometimes, with kindness. Not just to others, but to yourself.

I realised that being kind to myself, forgiving myself for bad days, praising myself for small wins, allowing space for fear without shame, that, was part of the attitude too. I couldn't control the cancer, but I could control how I treated me.

I'm not the same person I was before. That version of me is gone, and I've made peace with that (almost). But I've built someone new in their place, someone who's been through hell, and still gets up. Someone who still laughs, still loves, still chooses.

And that, in the end, has made all the difference.

David Jones-Stanley

The Pit.

I've already talked about how laughter, dear friends, and a bit of attitude helped me through my cancer treatment, one day at a time. But there was another "tool" I used, a survival mechanism. Something I don't talk about as easily, but one that kept me going.

I called it The Pit.

The Pit was where I put the things I couldn't carry in the moment. The thoughts too big, too scary, too heavy. The fears that crept in at 2 a.m. and threatened to smother me: Would I live to see my kids finish school? Would I see them fall in love, get married, have their own lives? Would my husband ever be the same again after watching me go through all of this? Would I even make it to my next birthday?

I couldn't deal with those questions. Not then. Not with the constant blood tests, the endless scans, the fatigue, the pain, the routines that were anything but routine. So, I put those thoughts somewhere.

I imagined The Pit as a kind of black hole, hovering just over my right shoulder. I could see the edge of it sometimes, you know, like when you catch a shadow in the corner of your eye, and when you turn, it's gone. It was always there. Quiet, patient, and bottomless.

And into it, I tossed everything I couldn't face. Not to ignore it, not really, but to survive. Because if I'd tried to hold it all at once, I'd have collapsed under the weight.

The Pit helped me stay upright. It let me get out of bed, go to appointments, smile for my kids, talk about treatment options, eat, walk, even laugh, all while a storm raged just out of sight.

It's not that I didn't feel. I felt everything. But I learned to postpone the worst of it. Because when you're fighting to live, you have to triage your emotions. You only deal with what you can, when you can.

But and this is important, The Pit had a price.

I knew that eventually, once the treatments slowed down and the worst of the storm passed, I'd have to go back. I'd have to look at what I'd buried. And that scared me. Because you don't get to drop fear, trauma, and grief into a pit forever and expect them to disappear. They wait. And when the noise dies down, when you finally get a moment of quiet, they come knocking.

That's when I realised, I needed help.

I found a counsellor. Someone I trusted. I told him about The Pit, and to his credit, he didn't flinch. He didn't try to give me a pep-talk or drag me toward the light. He understood what I meant. That I didn't need someone to fix the contents of the pit, I needed someone to help me go in, take a look around, and then get back out safely.

That was the danger. I could survive cancer and still get lost. Still drown in everything I'd been storing. I didn't want to live in The Pit. I just needed to visit it. Sort through it. Make sense of what I could and learn to live with what I couldn't.

That's what mental health support gave me. Not a magic cure, not instant relief, but the tools. The rope, the torch, the hand on my shoulder saying, "You can go in, and you can come back out."

Resilience isn't always about being strong. It's not always about "fighting" or "staying positive." Sometimes resilience is crying in the shower and still making yourself a cup of tea afterwards. It's booking a therapy session instead of pretending you're fine. It's admitting that surviving something doesn't mean you're healed.

There's this idea that once the treatment ends, you just bounce back. You ring the bell, throw a party, and carry on. But that's not the reality for many of us. Because while the world moves on, we're left holding all the pieces. The physical scars are healing, but the emotional ones? Those take time. And work. And help.

For a while, I felt guilty for needing that help. Like I should've been grateful just to be alive. And I was. But surviving isn't the same as thriving. And choosing to work on my mental health was the next brave thing I had to do.

What I've learned is this: it's okay to have a Pit. It's okay to not be okay. You're allowed to break down after the worst is over. You're allowed to need help, to ask for it, to accept it. That doesn't make you weak. That makes you wise.

So, if you've got a pit of your own, and I think many of us do, don't ignore it forever. You don't have to dive in all at once. But when you're ready, find someone who can help you shine a light in there. You might be surprised by what you find, the grief, yes, but also the strength. The survival. The parts of you that made it through.

I'm still working through mine. Still going in, still climbing back out. But now I know I can. And that, to me, is real resilience.

Part 5
Treatment and
Side Effects

"And there it was. Cancer.
Looking back at me in the mirror."

Tests, Scans, and the Waiting Game.

Waiting is something you get used to. Well, almost, there's a very particular type of anxiety that comes with waiting in the world of cancer. You're not waiting for a bus, or for your toast to pop up, or even for a delayed Amazon delivery. You're waiting for life-changing news, the kind that either steals your breath away or lets you breathe again, if only for a little while.

You're waiting for test results, to see the consultant, to hear if you're eligible for surgery, for phone calls to come (or not come), and above all else, you're waiting for this whole bloody thing to be over. Or at least to settle down into something resembling a new normal.

All of this is part of "the journey" (whatever that means). Personally, I think it's a word we use to make chaos sound like a guided tour.

But here's the twist: a small part of me appreciated the waiting. Not at the time, mind you. No, at the time it was like having your stomach permanently knotted and your brain buzzing with every possible outcome, good and bad. But on reflection? The waiting gave me space.

Space to plan. To think. To prepare for the "what ifs."

I used that time like mental prep work. I'd imagine: OK, its bad news, so that means this, or that... This is what I will do. This is who I will tell. This is what life might look like. I'd also allow myself to consider the good: it's good news, so now this can happen, maybe I can do that. The daydreams were both terrifying and comforting. They gave me some feeling of control.

And then, of course, came the tests.

Endoscopy (Gastroscopy) Ah yes, the glamorous start to it all. A thin, bendy camera goes down your throat. They offer sedation, but like a numpty, I declined. Instead, I lay there thinking, "Please let this be over soon," while tapping my fingers in a sort of Morse code for "get on with it."

Why it's done:
To see what the hell is going on in your oesophagus and stomach, and to take a biopsy if they spot anything that looks like it shouldn't be there.

CT scan of Chest and Abdomen. A giant polo mint that photocopies your insides. It's painless, over quickly, and comes with a delightful surprise: an injected dye that makes you feel like you've wet yourself. And even though they tell you this will happen, you still check.

Why it's done: To see if the cancer's crashed the party in your lungs or liver, or if it's sent invites to your lymph nodes. My results: T4/N1/M0. Not great.

PET-CT scan. Now these sounds very sci-fi. They inject you with radioactive sugar (which is very on-brand for my sweet tooth), tell you not to move or talk for 40 minutes, and then scan you. You lie there like a radioactive statue.

Why it's done: To catch sneaky little bits of cancer that don't show up on a regular CT. In my case, two hotspots lit up: one on my hip, one on my vocal cords. Cue mild (major) panic.

Endoscopic Ultrasound (EUS) Like the original endoscopy but with an added ultrasound probe. Given how "fun" the first one was, I went for the sedative this time. Smart move.

Why it's done: To measure how deep the tumour has grown into the oesophagus wall and check lymph nodes. Bonus: my T4 downgraded to T3. Hello, curative pathway. Cue massive relief.

Nasal Endoscopy (Nasendoscopy). Not usually on the oesophageal cancer playlist, but because my vocal cords lit up in the PET-CT, I got an extra one. A camera up the nose, down the back of the throat.

Why it's done: To rule out head and neck problems. Mine was all clear, probably just me yapping too much during the PET scan.

Staging Laparoscopy with Abdominal Wash Keyhole surgery to see if my cancer had had a wander around my abdomen. And yes, they actually "wash" your insides with saline to check for microscopic nasties.

Why it's done: To double, check if surgery is still a safe, curative option.

This was followed by my first "slap myself" moment. I got home, looked at the tiny 2-inch scar and thought, "This must be what a C-section feels like."

SLAP!

"Are you effing kidding me?" I said to myself, Women have humans pulled out of them. And I'm moaning about a keyhole scratch? From that day on, I made a rule: when I catch myself being dramatic, I give myself a little reality slap. (Don't worry, just metaphorical... mostly.)

Pre-Operative Fitness Tests, because surgery is a big deal, and they want to make sure your body can handle it. Cue an endless checklist:

ECG: Check the old ticker.

Blood tests: So many blood tests. I started to think I was part-time donating.

Lung function tests: Blow into a tube like you are inflating a bouncy castle.

Exercise tolerance: Can you walk without falling over? Excellent.

Why it's done: To make sure you won't keel over on the table. Fair enough.

Looking back, each of these scans and tests was a tick on an exceptionally long to do list. Each brought a wave of fear, hope, and sometimes laughter. And the waiting in between? Agonising, yes. But also, a strange kind of gift.

Time to plan.

Time to process.

Time to prepare.

And, in a twisted way, time to grow.

If you are reading this and you're in that waiting game right now, just know you are not alone. Keep breathing. Keep slapping yourself (metaphorically, please). Keep going. The next phone call might just be the one that shifts everything.

GULP

Chemo King.

Chemo King... that's what my dad used to call me. He took me to every appointment without fail. We were still recovering from the impact of COVID, so he wasn't allowed to sit with me inside the chemo unit. Instead, he made a ritual of it, newspaper under one arm, a hot coffee in hand, and endless patience as he waited for hours in the hospital car park while I sat hooked up to a drip full of poison, doing battle with cancer. Like a sentinel.

Funny thing about parents, they'll find any reason to be proud of you. And for my dad, this was it. He was proud of how I showed up, how I endured, how I kept going even when every part of me wanted to stop. Proud of my strength, my stubbornness, my humour. Proud of the way I wore my pain. He wasn't just watching me fight cancer, he was watching me win little battles every day. Hence, the Chemo King.

I prepared for chemo like I was going to war, but instead of a sword and shield, I had a pen and notebook, an iPad and phone, snacks and drinks, a hat and a scarf, and yes, God help me, a colouring book. I'd never coloured in my life, but someone swore by it, so into the bag it went. I was armed to the teeth with distraction.

Now, chemo isn't easy, no matter what Hollywood might try and tell you. The moment I sat in that chair and got hooked up, I could feel it. A cold wave crept up my spine, onto the back of my neck, and over my scalp like a ghost's hand. My lips went numb. My hands felt like blocks of ice. That coldness would stay with me like an unwelcome shadow.

Each session took about seven hours, but it felt like days. When I was finally done, they handed me a little bottle of "homework" a flask of chemo that I had to wear for 24 hours, connected to my body through a tube. I'd anticipated this and invested in a Lazy Boy recliner so I could sleep without yanking it out during the night. That chair ended up being one of the best purchases of my life.

The side effects came in fast. Within hours of my first round, I felt it: cold sensitivity, nausea, tingling. But I held up okay, at first. The second round was worse, vomiting and the start of some hair loss. By the third round, I was bald, my beard gone, frequent nosebleeds, and then it hit me: fatigue. Not tiredness. Not sleepiness. This was something else. Something that felt primal. Like gravity had doubled overnight and I was pinned to my bed by the weight of my own body.

That was the first time I truly understood why people say, "I can't do this anymore." For the first time, I thought maybe I couldn't either.

It was a wake-up call. A moment where I realised maybe I wouldn't do "anything" to survive. Maybe there were limits. You go into chemo convinced, absolutely certain that you'll do whatever it takes to win. And then BAM! the treatment hits back. And you start to wonder whether you're strong enough. That was one of the only times in my life I used the word hope. I hoped I was stronger than the poison they were pumping into me.

One of the hardest parts was losing my beard. Not because I was vain. I'd had that beard for 18 years, my kids had never seen me without one. Sure, I was already thinning up top, but the beard? That was me. When it went, I didn't just lose hair, I lost a part of my identity.

People would say, "Don't worry, you'll be fine, you see loads of bald men." And they're right. But this wasn't about looking bald. This wasn't vanity.

No one told me that losing your hair when you have cancer, cancer you can't see, suddenly becomes the moment you do see it.

Oesophageal cancer hides inside you. It's not a lump you can point to, not a tumour on the outside. It lives deep down. I never saw it. Not really. Until I lost my hair. My beard. My eyebrows. And there it was. Cancer. Looking back at me in the mirror.

I remember staring into my own reflection and whispering,

"Oh. There you are."

It wasn't just me anymore. It was me with cancer, and I finally had the face to match.

.

GULP

David Jones-Stanley

Part 6
Surgery and
Recovery

"I think about death more than
life.
And that's OK."

Sliced and diced.

The title of this chapter might sound harsh, but honestly, it's the only way I can describe how I felt about the operation. If you're squeamish, you might want to skip this one. But if you're curious about what really happens when they cut you open and rearrange your insides, pull up a chair, I'm going to tell it straight.

I knew from the beginning that I'd be having open surgery rather than keyhole. Why? I'm still not entirely sure. Even after speaking to my surgeon many times since, I've never asked. Maybe I didn't want to hear the answer. What I did know was that the "preparation" part felt deceptively straightforward: fitness tests, conversations with the pre-op team, and a run-through of the logistics.

The mechanics were explained in detail, what they'd do, where they'd cut, how long I'd be in hospital. But nothing, and I mean nothing, prepared me for the moment I'd look down afterwards and saw a body I barely recognised.

The day of the surgery was like checking into a very grim hotel, no breakfast, an unflattering gown, and DVT socks that are about as comfortable as wet cardboard. My husband dropped me off at 7 a.m. and drove away, not allowed to stay because of hospital policy. I walked into the ward with my overnight bag, feeling strangely calm and oddly aware of the grey, wet Manchester morning outside. Miserable weather. At least I'd miss most of it.

One by one, the cast of characters arrived: nurses, doctors, anaesthetists, research assistants. All smiling, all armed with clipboards, all asking for my consent. Now, they asked me, "Do you consent to the surgery?" but what I really heard was: "Do you want a chance at living?" My answer was an easy yes, every time.

By 8:30 a.m., I was changed into my gown and socks, pacing the room because I refused to sit on the bed. Then came the call: they were ready for me. I walked into the anaesthetic room to set up my epidural, and that's where the fun began. Apparently, my spine didn't want to cooperate. Several attempts later, a more experienced consultant was called in to have a go at it! Meanwhile, a nurse zipped around me like a caffeinated bee, sticking patches on my chest, setting up cannulas, attaching tubes. Finally, they gave up on guesswork, wheeled in a portable Xray machine, positioned me face-down for repeated scans until the needle was in exactly the right spot.

A quick injection. Mask over my face. Darkness. Eleven hours gone.

When I woke up... let's just say I wasn't exactly Mr. Sunshine. I've only had a general anaesthetic twice before, once I woke up angry, once I was fine. This time? Full Incredible Hulk mode. Two large men were standing at the end of my bed, probably to make sure I didn't start flipping trolleys. When I realised the Hulk had gone, I asked, "Was I angry?" and saw the faint smiles that told me yes, I had been.

It was 1 a.m. when they wheeled me into ICU. My surgeon, who had seen me at 7:30 that morning, was still there, calmly checking on me. He'd phoned my husband around 11 p.m. to say the surgery had gone well, although it had taken longer because, as he put it, "there was a lot of him to get through." Charming.

The first thing I remember feeling was nausea. Not pain, just that awful urge to vomit, which is particularly worrying when you've just had your oesophagus stitched to your stomach. "Protect the join" became my mantra. The next morning, after a restless night, I finally managed to look down.

The scar surprised me. I'd assumed it would run straight up and down, but instead, there was a 14-inch slash across me from side-to-side. I couldn't see the matching one on my back, but I could feel the tubes, all 14 of them. Chest drains, feeding lines, catheters. I looked like I'd been wired up for a NASA mission.

No pain yet, thank you epidural, but moving felt like I'd been hit by two buses, a lorry, and a moped for good measure. Getting from bed to chair required three people. Still, I managed it on day one, which apparently is a big win in surgery land.

The pain came later, along with the morphine drip. Morphine is brilliant at numbing pain, but it's equally brilliant at making you hallucinate and keeping you from sleeping. The next two days were a blur of physio-led walks, strange dreams, and my husband and dad visiting. They were the only two people I allowed in. I refused to let my children visit ICU. I didn't want their memory of me to be tubes, drains, and pale, post-op Dad.

There's a photo on my phone from the morning after surgery. I've only looked at it a handful of times. Even now, it's hard to see myself like that, stitched up, and utterly changed.

I'd gone in thinking surgery was the final hurdle. I woke up realising it was only the start of a whole new fight.

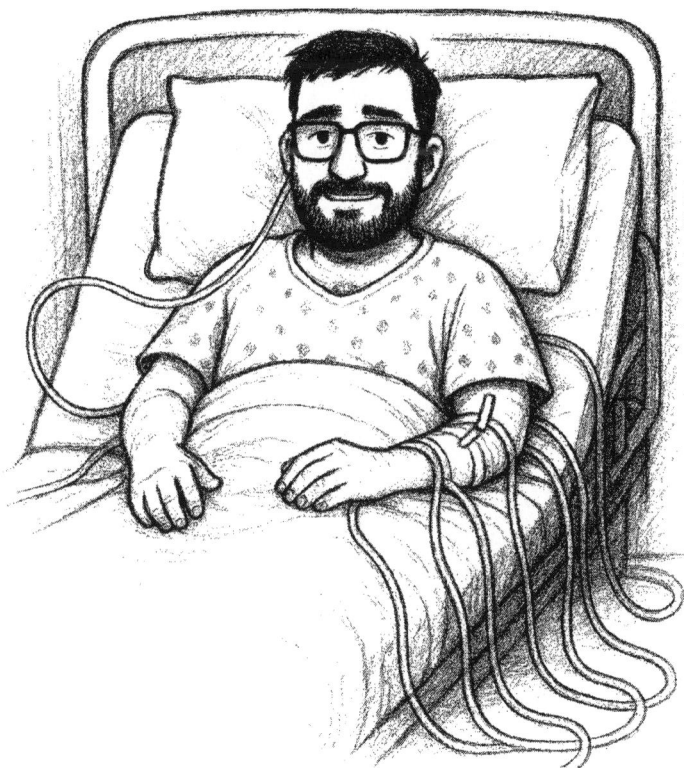

Tubes, tubes and tubes.

No, I'm not talking about the Jubilee or Circle lines. I'm talking about the 14 tubes that were inserted into various parts of my body. Some were there to pump things in, some to drain things out, and some just to make me look like an extra from a low, budget sci-fi movie.

Let's take stock.

Stuff going in:

Oxygen: Technically not a tube, but definitely something I relied on. For me, it had to be a mask rather than a nasal cannula because, apparently, I'm a mouth breather. Who knew? Well, I soon knew when my oxygen levels dropped during sleep, and I was abruptly awoken at 1 a.m. by alarms blaring and a team of people surrounding my bed like I'd just flatlined in a soap opera.

Central line: To administer medication directly into a big vein. The "main motorway" for all the good stuff.

Peripheral IV: Because apparently one entry point for fluids wasn't enough.

Jejunostomy feeding tube: My gourmet dining experience for the next six months. This was the last tube to leave me, like a clingy houseguest who doesn't get the hint.

Epidural catheter: Pumped pain meds straight into my spine. Glorious.

Morphine line: Because sometimes, epidural alone just doesn't cut it.

Stuff coming out:

Arterial line: Constant blood pressure and blood gas monitoring.

Nasogastric tube: The Hoover for my stomach, keeping it free of unwanted fluids.

Chest drain 1 (Upper right)

Chest drain 2 (Lower right)

Chest drain 3 (Upper left)

Chest drain 4 (Lower left) Yes, four chest drains. At one point, I felt like I should be charging rent.

Urinary catheter: The kind of "convenience" you're grateful for... until they take it out.

Wound drain: Collected anything that dared leak from the main surgical site.

Part of knowing I was getting better was the gradual removal of each of these tubes. We started with the chest drains, which felt like a milestone.

After a few days, the rest came out in quick succession.

Now, here's my theory: I'm fairly certain that the urinary catheter is removed at the exact moment your body decides to flush out every last drop of fluid it's been hoarding. The second mine came out, I was up to the toilet every fifteen minutes. Maybe it was a medical necessity. Maybe it was a clever way to make sure I started walking again. Either way, it worked.

I remember each and every one of these tubes, what they did, how they felt, and the strange comfort of knowing they had a purpose. None of them were particularly painful, although one chest drain did put up a fight on its way out.

If I had to describe the overall look, I'd say: imagine a KerPlunk game, only instead of marbles, it's me, with tubes poking out in every direction. I must have been quite a sight. I sometimes think it was more shocking for my visitors than it was for me.

If I can give any advice about tubes, it's this: learn what they're there for, celebrate each one as it comes out, and be thankful that they never go back in. Because each tube leaving is a little victory, and those victories add up to recovery.

The early days.

The early days following surgery are hard. Even though I was told it would be difficult and that recovery would be hard, I wasn't prepared for the size of the climb, I felt like I would never make it, it was too hard. But each day I walked further, I was able to talk more, I was less tired, I was able to laugh with the nursing team, I was slowly becoming me again (albeit a different me.)

After the 3rd day I was able to drink some clear fluids; plain water from the tap has never tasted so good. I was still very continuous that I had this new join where my oesophagus attached to my new stomach, and I was very aware that there are quite often complications with this join, so I took drinking very slowly, 30ml only, and every drop of liquid in and out was carefully measured.

Before surgery my surgeon had gone through with me the "plan", it was a 9-day plan laid out in excel. When he showed me the excel spreadsheet in his office a few weeks earlier, I knew this was the guy for my surgery! It was a detailed description of what each day's aims were, walking, tubes, drinking etc, and this was printed off for me and put at the end of my bed, so I could see what

I was going to be doing and could see that I was on track. Of cause all good plans can have bumps in the road, and after day 2 my temperature started to spike, fever, and pain, and my blood indicators started to spike. At this point there were a few possible causes, one was a chest infection, not uncommon given that your chest is opened up for several hours, the second, and possible the riskier was a failure of the join, the one thing that I had dreaded more than anything else. So, I was immediately X-rayed at the bedside, put on IV antibiotics, and send for a CT scan. During the CT scan I was placed on my back, laid out flat, something that I am not great at doing, and with a mouth full of fluid I was asked to swallow at exactly the right time so they could track it on the CT as the fluid passing through the new join. As I lay there I thought, "this is it – this is how I'm going to die, with a mouth full of liquid!", of cause, I didn't, and thankfully the join was perfect. The chest infection did go away after a few days, but it added 3 days to my stay.

I stayed in ICU for 5 days, then was moved to the high observation ward, I stayed there for a few more days and finally was moved to a more general surgical ward. By this time, I was up and about, walking independently and drinking as and when I felt like, tea, juice, and then soft meals. I'm not sure if it was my taste buds, or the fact that I handed eaten anything "real" in weeks, but the first few bites made me feel so ill – but I persevered and managed to eat some food (well, mush really) before I was eventually told I could go home.

GULP

Learning to live.

When the Bus misses you, you keep watching the road! I think about death more than I think about life, and it took me nearly three years to understand that's OK.

After surviving stage 3 oesophageal cancer, for three years now, eight rounds of chemo and one of the most invasive and dangerous surgeries you can have (an oesophagectomy), I set about learning to live again. Hopefully better than before, and I say that not as someone who didn't live well before, but as someone who now truly understands that life isn't forever.

The challenge, is that cancer doesn't exactly let you "move on." The recurrence rates for some are high, and for me the five, and ten-year survival statistics are brutal. Even when your body is healing, your mind still knows the odds. It's like living with a quiet shadow that occasionally steps right into the sunlight to remind you it's there.

People often expect cancer survivors to see the world differently, and I mean "better". The sky should be bluer, the flowers should smell sweeter, and every moment should be more precious. And yes, sometimes that's true. But it's also true that when you've nearly been killed by a bus, you don't just start enjoying the scenery, you become hyper-aware of the road.

In the first year after treatment, I thought I was doing survivorship wrong. I wasn't walking around in a permanent state of gratitude. I didn't want to seize every single day. And despite people telling me I was an inspiration, I instead kept thinking about death. About recurrence. About how fragile all of this really is. I thought that meant I was failing at living.

And then I remembered The Pit.

During treatment, The Pit was my mental storage unit for fear, the place I put the thoughts I couldn't handle in the moment. Will I live to see my kids grow up? Will my husband ever be the same? Will this pain ever stop? All of it went into The Pit, tucked away so I could focus on getting through each day.

But now treatment has ended, I realise that The Pit didn't vanish. It was still there, just behind my right shoulder, holding everything I had avoided. In those first months after chemo and surgery, I started dipping back into it, not all at once, but enough to see what I'd buried, and with some assistance. And what I realised was that my constant thoughts about death weren't new. They'd been sitting in The Pit the whole time.

The difference now was that I wasn't afraid to look at them.

Over time, I began to see that thinking about death wasn't me being morbid, it was me being aware. It was the same mental habit that had helped me survive treatment, just in a different form. Back then, I used The Pit to compartmentalise fear so I could keep going. Now, I let some of that fear stay in the open because it pushes me to live more deliberately.

That awareness has changed me. It's made me stop putting off conversations I want to have. It's made me less interested in small talk and more interested in saying what I really mean. It's made me value my time, and other people's, in a way I never had before.

I'm not here to pretend that cancer is a gift, it's not. But it has been a teacher. And one of its hardest lessons was learning that living with death in the back of your mind doesn't mean you're not living. It can mean you're living more honestly.

So yes, I think about death more than life. And that's OK. Because if that awareness pushes me to show up fully, to stop wasting time, and to treat the people I love like I might not get another chance, then I'm fine with that.

It's not about beating the bus. It's about noticing the road, every single day.

GULP

Part 7
Life After Cancer

"I may not be who I was before but that's OK. That version of me didn't know how strong I was. This one does."

Life After Cancer
Different, Not Worse

Life after cancer isn't about "getting back to normal." There is no going back, the landscape changes, and so do you. But different doesn't have to mean worse. It goes without saying that going through cancer will change you. People tell me it's an awakening, a moment where you suddenly see the world for how it "really" is. I'm not sure I had that epiphany, there was no beam of light through the clouds, no booming voice from above. But I did experience change. To every part of my life.

I've been through change before. We all have. Jobs, houses, relationships, family. I've been a son, a partner, a father, a husband. But until cancer, most change in my life had been change I either wanted or at least had some control over. And usually, it came one at a time.

Cancer isn't like that. Cancer is the table-flipping, furniture-rearranging, "Oh, you liked your life how it was? Tough" kind of change. And it doesn't just hit one part of you. It hits all of you. All at once.

I don't want this to sound like a moan. It's not. This is just the reality of what happens, and in some ways, it's not all bad. There are many changes, let's start with the Physical Stuff...

The big one: weight loss.

Before my diagnosis, I was on the Slimming World diet plan, and thought I was doing well, although, looking back, I suspect it wasn't the meal plan so much as the tumour giving me a helping hand (cheers for the certificates, Cancer).

By the time I went in for surgery, I was over 130 kg. After surgery, I lost 38 kg without even trying. That's not a "before and after" that's an entire teenager gone.

I didn't diet. I couldn't. I had a jejunostomy feeding tube put in during surgery and lived on daily feeds that eventually shifted to overnight feeds alongside soups, soft foods, and later, real solids. My muscles melted away along with the fat, and exercise became essential just to build myself back up.

Walking became my recovery ritual: first to the end of the drive, then the corner, then the top of the street. My lungs, still sulking from surgery, made each step feel like I was climbing hills I couldn't see. Even stairs became events.

GULP

When I came out of hospital, I had several wounds to take care of. The community team offered to come to me, at home, but I insisted on going to the clinic every day. Partly because I'm stubborn. Mostly because it forced me to get up, wash, dress, and leave the house. Poor Dad became my chauffeur again, but it was better than sitting at home stewing in my own sweat.

The wardrobe purge was almost a ceremony. My old clothes hung off me like I'd been playing dress-up in my dad's suit cupboard. Suits, shirts, trousers, jumpers, all gone to charity.

Shopping wasn't exactly my favourite sport, but suddenly I could buy clothes anywhere. Dropping ten inches off your waist means you don't have to head straight for the "back of the rail" section where they keep the tent-sized jeans. My wallet hated it, but I have to admit... I did enjoy becoming a reluctant fashionista.

Sleeping became a new challenge. I couldn't lie flat anymore without risking acid reflux that could wake me up choking at 2 a.m. Sleeping slightly propped up isn't natural, at least, not for me. I eventually bought a wedge pillow, and it became my nightly reminder that I'm not quite the same as before. Of all the things I've lost, sleeping flat on my back is one of the strangest to miss.

Bending over also became a tactical manoeuvre. Bend too quickly after eating and, thanks to my new plumbing, whatever's in my stomach might make a reappearance. Let's just say gravity is less my friend these days.

And then there's the mirror. For months after treatment, I didn't recognise the man looking back. I knew it was me, obviously, but my mental picture of myself hadn't caught up with the actual reflection. It was always a bit of a double-take moment, like bumping into an old school friend you didn't realise had moved into your bathroom.

The physical changes are only part of it. The emotional and psychological ones run deeper.

Before all this, people would probably describe me as loving, caring, devoted, and loyal, but also blunt and very black-and-white. I've always been the "sit down, tell me your problem, and I'll give you a 10-point plan" guy. No fuss, no dithering, no unnecessary tears.

Now? Let's just say the emotional side has moved up from the basement to the ground floor. I'm much more aware of life's limits. And I've got far less patience for people who waste my time.

Before cancer, I'd happily wait for someone to make a decision. Now, if you hesitate, I'll make it for you, and dam quickly. And I won't apologise.

The people around me are still adjusting to this new version of me. Some like it. Some don't. But honestly? That's for them to deal with. Cancer changes you in ways you can't control and often can't predict. Some of it's hard. Some of it's inconvenient. But some of it, if you let it, can be oddly liberating.

I may not be who I was before but that's OK. That version of me didn't know how strong I was. This one does.

Food glorious food.

If there's one topic that comes up at every support group, online forum, and conversation with every clinician - it's food. Food is such a central part of our lives. We use it to celebrate, to commiserate, to bribe our kids into behaving, and sometimes as a reason to get people together when we can't think of anything else to do. It's woven into family traditions, birthdays, weddings, funerals, and for me, pre-cancer, it was pure joy.

I was a big foodie. I loved to cook, I loved to eat, and if you came to my house for dinner, you didn't just leave full, you left questioning whether you'd ever need to eat again. But now? My relationship with food is... complicated. Think "it's not you, it's me" but with chicken soup.

From the moment I slurped my first soup in ICU, I realised eating would never be the same. It wasn't just about what I could eat, it was about learning to eat all over again. After surgery, they'd cut my nerve, which meant my hunger signals went away, permanently. For some people, appetite comes back. For me, it didn't.

So now, I don't want food, I have to schedule it. I can manage about 200g of food per sitting (think a good handful) and I need to do that 6 or 7 times a day. That means eating has gone from a pleasure to a task, almost like brushing your teeth, but with an added "I hope this doesn't cause dumping syndrome." Question running through my brain.

Because my portions are small, every meal has to work hard. I can't "waste" a meal on something that tastes nice but gives me no nutrition. Sure, a bowl of carrots might look virtuous, but at 67 calories and 1g of protein, it's not going to help me rebuild muscle. So, I'll choose 200g of chicken instead - 340 calories and 20g of protein, because in my new food world, maths matters more than cravings.

Don't get me wrong, I still enjoy some of the things I used to eat, I'm just a lot more strategic about it. Think less "what do I fancy?" and more "what will keep me upright and moving today?"

Eating out used to be one of my favourite things. Now? Not so much. First, there's choosing something I can eat without triggering dumping syndrome. Then there's the ritual of being served a giant plate of food, picking at a third of it, and being asked by the waiter, every time, "Is everything alright with your meal, sir?"

I used to launch into an explanation about surgery, stomach size, and medical stuff, but now I just smile and say, "It's lovely, I just don't eat much." They usually nod politely but I can see in their eyes they're thinking, "Sure, mate."

And then there's the awkwardness of being the first to finish... or rather, the first to stop eating while everyone else is still on their starters. It took a while, but I've learned to focus on the conversation, not the food.

Now, we have to talk about dumping.

Terrible name. Even worse experience. Technically it's called Rapid Gastric Emptying, which somehow sounds both more medical and more unpleasant. It happens when food (especially sugary or fatty food) rushes from your stomach into your small intestine too quickly.

The first time it happened to me; I was about two weeks home from hospital. I fancied a slice of cheesecake, one of my pre-surgery favourites. I had a small slice. It was delicious. For about 20 minutes.

Then came the wave, sweating, dizziness, nausea, stomach cramps, and a bathroom sprint that would've impressed an Olympic athlete. After 20 minutes of that joy, I collapsed into bed and slept for hours, feeling like I'd just done a marathon... through treacle. Cheesecake was officially off the menu.

Over time, I've learned what triggers it for me. High sugar? Nope. Processed fats? Forget it. Creamy, rich desserts? Only if I've completely forgotten I like living. Natural sugars and good fats tend to be kinder, but even then, it's a gamble.

And just when I think I've cracked the code, I'll get hit with dumping from something I've eaten a dozen times before without issue. It's trial and error. Mostly error.

The hardest part of all this isn't the mechanics of eating, it's the loss of the joy I used to get from food. But over time, I've found small wins: a perfectly poached egg, a delicious, steamed fish dish, a tiny scoop of ice cream that I can handle.

Food may not be the love affair it once was, but it's still a relationship worth tending to, just with a lot more boundaries.

And if nothing else, it's given me one undeniable truth: cheesecake is a liar.

GULP

Part 8
Looking back, and forward.

When I look back, I realise something important: I never really expected life to go "back to normal,"

GULP

LOOKING
BACK

Looking back.

Oone of the most common, and possibly most baffling, questions I get asked is: "If you had to, would you do it all again?" I always answer yes. Not because I loved it, not because I think chemo should be marketed as a spa experience, but because at the time, the question isn't about whether you want surgery and treatment. It's about whether you want to live. And when you're faced with that choice, there's no debate. You choose life. Every time.

If we're being honest, it's a bit of a silly question, in the same way asking someone who was saved from drowning if they'd accept the life ring again is silly. Of course they would.

The more interesting question people ask is: "Would you do anything differently?"

And here's where I pause. I think I did pretty well, all things considered. I kept working for as long as I could. I even managed to get promoted after coming back, not bad for someone who spent months looking like a medical supply store on legs. I kept my family together, held myself together (most of the time), and came out the other side... different, yes, slightly damaged, more emotional, less tolerant of nonsense, but here. And "here" is a win.

When I look back, I realise something important: I never really expected life to go "back to normal," but I think a part of me assumed it would feel the same eventually. It doesn't. And that's not bad, it's just different.

I eat differently. Not worse. Not better. Just... differently. Food is fuel first now, pleasure second. The old me would have demolished a roast dinner the size of a car tyre and gone back for pudding. The new me eats 200 grams at a time, six or seven times a day, because that's what my body allows. I've made peace with it. And I've learned that enjoying a meal doesn't have to mean eating a lot, sometimes it's just about being able to eat it without spending the next two hours in "dumping" hell.

I move differently. Recovery taught me that stairs are an extreme sport, that walking to the end of the street is sometimes the victory, and that even after the tubes are gone, the body still remembers. My lungs, my scars, my stamina, all altered. But they're mine.

I sleep differently. Gone is the luxury of lying flat on my back without thinking about reflux, joins, and gravity. My wedge pillow is my nightly reminder that I'm not the same person I was before surgery. It's a small change, but it's symbolic, I wake up every morning knowing my body has new rules now.

And I think differently. Before cancer, I knew I was mortal, in the same abstract way we all do, but I didn't feel it. Now, I think about death more than life. That used to bother me. Survivorship is meant to come with a Hollywood-style glow, right? The skies are bluer, flowers smell sweeter, and every moment is precious.

Except... that's not quite how it works. When you've been nearly killed by the proverbial bus, you don't just admire the sky, you keep an eye on the road. Thinking about death doesn't make me morbid; it makes me deliberate. It reminds me that time is the one resource you never get back.

The Pit, my mental black hole where I stored my worst fears during treatment, still exists. I don't visit it often now, but knowing it's there is strangely comforting. It's a reminder that I've faced those thoughts before and survived them.

There are things I might tweak in hindsight, maybe I'd have asked more questions about surgery, maybe I'd have been gentler with myself in the worst weeks of chemo. But the big picture? No, I wouldn't change my approach. I got through it in the only way I knew how, by planning when I could, laughing when I could, and just keeping moving when I couldn't do either.

So, here's the truth:
Would I do it again? Yes.
Would I change much? No.
Would I trade the perspective, grit, and stubborn appreciation
I've gained? Absolutely not.

I am different now, physically, mentally, emotionally. But I'm still here. And here is good. Here means I get to be with my family. Here means I can plan next week. Here means there is still a road ahead, and I'm walking it, one deliberate step at a time.

GULP

LOOKING
FORWARD

The future of cancer care.

If there's one thing I learned from this whole nightmare, it's that cancer care doesn't stand still. What I went through was the best treatment available at the time, surgery, chemotherapy, endless scans and check-ups, but even as I was having it, there was talk of what's coming next. And that gives me hope, not just for me, but for the next person who hears those three words: "you have cancer".

One of the biggest changes is the rise of genomics and biomarkers. For years, cancer treatment was a bit of a blunt instrument. You had surgery if they could cut it out. You had chemo if they couldn't. Radiotherapy if they thought it might help. It was very much one-size-fits-all. But here's the truth: cancers aren't all the same, even when they've got the same name. Two people can both have oesophageal cancer, but their tumours can behave completely differently.

That's where genomics comes in. Scientists now have the ability to map the genetic profile of a tumour, to look at the unique DNA changes and mutations that are driving it. It's like lifting the bonnet of a car and realising that not every engine fault needs the same spanner. Some need rewiring. Some need oil. Some, let's be honest, need a brand-new engine.

I was lucky enough to have my tumour genomically profiled. At the time, I didn't fully grasp what that meant. To me, it sounded like something out of a sci-fi film. But when the results came back, they gave me something I hadn't had for months: reassurance. What the profiling showed was that my cancer was the "type" most likely to respond to the treatment plan I was already on. In other words, the gruelling chemotherapy and surgery weren't just educated guesses, the science backed it up. For once, I didn't feel like a lab rat. I felt like a patient on the right road.

That reassurance was huge. When you're being pumped full of drugs that make your hair fall out, your appetite disappears and your body ache in places you didn't know existed, the least you want is to know it's the right poison. Genomic profiling gave me that peace of mind.

And the truth is, this is only the beginning. In the future, cancer treatment will be less about throwing everything at the wall to see what sticks, and more about precision medicine, targeting the right drug to the right tumour at the right time. Biomarkers, tiny measurable signs in blood, tissue, or even your breath, are already helping doctors predict how a cancer might behave, how aggressive it is, and which treatments will (or won't) work. Imagine a world where instead of waiting months to see if chemotherapy has shrunk a tumour, you could know in advance whether it's likely to help at all. That's not science fiction anymore, it's happening.

Even beyond treatment, genomics could change the way we detect cancer. Right now, diagnosis often comes late, when symptoms can't be ignored. But with new blood tests that can pick up fragments of tumour DNA floating around (so-called "liquid biopsies"), there's the potential to catch cancer earlier, when it's far easier to treat, or even prevent it altogether.

Don't get me wrong, this won't happen overnight. The NHS is brilliant but also stretched, and rolling out cutting-edge science to every patient will take time. There will still be frustration, delays, and moments when the system feels like a maze. But the direction of travel is clear. Cancer care is shifting from generic treatments to personalised journeys, tailored to the individual, not just the disease.

For me, knowing my tumour had been profiled, and that the science matched the plan, gave me something priceless: confidence. Confidence that the pain, the nausea, the scars, were all part of the right fight. And that's what the future of cancer care promises, less guesswork, more certainty, and hopefully, more survivors sitting where I am now, able to write their story.

Because if I've learned anything, it's this: cancer is a bastard, but knowledge is its match. And the more we understand about what makes each tumour tick, the better our chances of beating it.

GULP

David Jones-Stanley

My Top Tips.

Top 10 Tips for Anyone facing cancer (from someone who's been there)

1. Trust your gut (literally for me!). If something feels wrong in your body, don't ignore it. Push for answers. You know yourself better than anyone.

2. Be your own project manager. Keep a notebook or use your phone to write down names, dates, results, and questions. The system is big and messy; you need to stay on top of it.

3. Ask questions. Then ask again. Don't nod along if you don't understand. Say: "Can you explain that in plain English?" Good doctors will respect you for it.

4. Remember: it's your body, your journey. Doctors are experts in medicine; you're the expert in you. Speak up if something doesn't feel right.

5. Laugh whenever you can. Humour won't cure cancer, but it makes the unbearable bearable. Find one thing each day that makes you smile...it's rebellion in its purest form.

6. Not everyone will stick around, and that's okay. Some friends will disappear. Others will surprise you with their kindness. Focus on the ones who show up.

7. Choose your moments to share. You don't owe your story to everyone. Some days you'll want to talk; other days you'll just want to talk about the weather. Both are valid. Seeking professional help can also be helpful – counselling, support groups are great places to start.

8. Stay curious because knowledge is power. Read, learn, and if possible, get genomic profiling or biomarker testing. The more you know, the more confident you'll feel in your treatment plan.

9. Take control where you can. Cancer takes a lot out of you, but small things like bringing someone to appointments, deciding how you get results, setting your own pace that help you feel less like a passenger.

10. Life after cancer is different, not worse. Recovery takes time. Food, routines, energy levels may all shift. But it doesn't mean life is over, it's just a new version of it.

David Jones-Stanley

Turning survival into support.

When the dust started to settle after treatment, I found myself at a crossroads. Do I try to push cancer into a dark cupboard, lock the door, and pretend it never happened? Or do I take everything I'd been through: the scans, the swearing, the waiting, the tubes, the laughter, the tears, and use it to help someone else?

Writing this book is part of my answer to that question. It wasn't easy. Reliving the moments I'd much rather forget, the nights staring at the ceiling wondering if I'd ever see my kids grow up, the sheer indignity of trying to eat a sandwich and ending up in tears, it's not exactly the stuff you want to put down on paper. But I kept thinking back to that support group, those newly diagnosed faces staring at me with the same look I once had, fear, confusion, desperation for something real. And I thought, maybe my story could be that something real for someone else.

That's why I wrote Gulp. Not as a glossy "inspiration" piece or a medical textbook, but as the truth, warts and all. Because when I was first diagnosed, that's what I wanted most, honesty.

And if my honesty helps even one person feel less alone, then dragging myself back through the memories was worth it.

I've also found that sharing my story has helped me. It's strange but giving my cancer journey a purpose has softened some of its edges. Instead of just being something that happened to me, it's become something I can do something with. I've worked with charities, spoken at events, joined pathway boards to influence how we are cared for, and helped shape awareness campaigns. Each time I put myself out there, it costs me something, energy, emotion, a little vulnerability, but it also gives something back. A sense of connection. A feeling that the bastard of a disease didn't get the last word.

Now, let me be clear: you don't owe anyone your story. If you want to slam the book shut on cancer, never talk about it again, and get on with your life, that's absolutely fine. In fact, I completely understand. Going public isn't for everyone, and healing sometimes means walking away.

But if you do feel able to share, whether it's writing a blog, speaking at a group, joining a patient panel, or even just telling your mate down the pub, I'd encourage you to try because your story is powerful. Not polished, not perfect, not sugar-coated, just yours. And for someone else out there, it could be exactly what they need to hear.

Supporting others doesn't mean you become "the cancer person" forever. It doesn't define you, and it doesn't erase the rest of who you are. What it does is offer a way to turn something painful into something useful. To make meaning out of chaos. To create hope where, once upon a time, there was none.

For me, that's been healing in its own way. Cancer changed my life, yes, but choosing to share my story has allowed me to change other lives too. And that, more than anything, makes me feel like I've wrestled back a bit of control.

So, whether you decide to put your story out there or keep it close, know this: both choices are valid. Both choices are brave. And both choices belong to you.

GULP

Common terms you may come across.

Abbreviation, Meaning and Why it matters.

CT: Computed Tomography (scan)
Detailed imaging used to see tumours and check spread.

PET: Positron Emission Tomography (scan)
Detects active cancer cells in the body. Often combined with CT.

MRI: Magnetic Resonance Imaging
Imaging technique that shows soft tissue detail without radiation.

GP: General Practitioner
Your first point of contact in the NHS.

CNS: Clinical Nurse Specialist
Key contact for cancer patients, often your "go-to" person.

MDT: Multidisciplinary Team

GULP

Group of specialists (surgeons, oncologists, radiologists, nurses) who plan your care together.

NHS: National Health Service
The UK healthcare system providing cancer treatment.

Dx: Diagnosis
Short-hand in medical notes for when cancer is identified.

Tx: Treatment
Used for all forms of treatment: chemo, radiotherapy, surgery.

Rx: Prescription
Shorthand for medicines prescribed.

Chemo: Chemotherapy
Cancer-killing drugs, often given in cycles.

RT (or XRT): Radiotherapy
Treatment using high-energy radiation to destroy cancer cells.

Neo-adjuvant: Before main treatment

Often chemo or radiotherapy given before surgery to shrink tumours.

Adjuvant: After main treatment
Therapy given post-surgery to reduce recurrence risk.

Recurrence: Return of cancer
When cancer comes back after treatment.

Metastasis (Mets): Spread of cancer
When cancer cells move to other parts of the body.

Biomarker: Biological marker
A test (blood, tissue, genetic) that helps guide treatment.

Genomic Profiling: DNA testing of tumour
Identifies mutations and helps tailor treatment.

QoL: Quality of Life
How treatment and illness impact day-to-day living.

Palliative Care: Symptom-focused care

Supportive care aimed at comfort, not cure.

Survivorship: Life after cancer
The phase of living beyond treatment, adjusting to a new normal.

David Jones-Stanley

"If you're the next poor bastard who's just been told you have cancer, know this... you're not alone, you're allowed to be scared as hell, and if you make it through, life might be different... but you'll still be here."

David.

GULP

David Jones-Stanley

GULP

Printed in Dunstable, United Kingdom